Elizabeth I

Queen of England 1558–1603

Written by Jonathan Melmoth   Illustrated by Jennie Poh

Author Jonathan Melmoth
Illustrator Jennie Poh
Subject Consultant Dr. Ellie Woodacre
Editor Rea Pikula
Designer Sadie Thomas at LS Design
Senior Editor Marie Greenwood
US Senior Editor Shannon Beatty
Additional Illustration James Hearne
Additional Design Charlotte Jennings
Additional Editorial Becca Arlington
Jacket Coordinator Elin Woosnam
Managing Editor Gemma Farr
Managing Art Editor Diane Peyton Jones
Production Editor Dragana Puvacic
Production Controller Rebecca Parton
Publisher Francesca Young
Art Director Mabel Chan
Managing Director Sarah Larter

First American Edition, 2024
Published in the United States by DK Publishing,
a division of Penguin Random House LLC
1745 Broadway, 20th Floor, New York, NY 10019

Copyright © 2024 Dorling Kindersley Limited
24 25 26 27 28 10 9 8 7 6 5 4 3 2 1
001–341128–Jul/2024

A catalog record for this book
is available from the Library of Congress.
ISBN 978-0-7440-9960-7

DK books are available at special discounts when purchased
in bulk for sales promotions, premiums, fund-raising, or
educational use. For details, contact: DK Publishing Special
Markets, 1745 Broadway, 20th Floor, New York, NY 10019
SpecialSales@dk.com

Printed and bound in China

www.dk.com

Contents

The Tudor family

Elizabeth was the fifth and final monarch from the Tudor family. They seized the English crown in 1485 when Elizabeth's grandfather Henry VII, from the House of Lancaster, defeated Richard III, from the House of York, at the Battle of Bosworth Field. Altogether, the Tudors ruled for more than 100 years.

House of Tudor

Henry VII
1457–1509

Henry Tudor had a claim to the throne through his great-great-grandfather, John of Gaunt, who was the son of King Edward III.

Arthur Tudor
1486–1502

As Henry VII's eldest son, Arthur was heir to the throne. He married Katherine of Aragon, but died, aged just 15.

Margaret Tudor
1489–1541

Margaret's marriage to the Scottish king helped the Tudors strengthen ties with the Scots, although they still fought against the English.

James IV of Scotland
1473–1513

James was a successful king, but he was killed by Henry VIII's forces at the Battle of Flodden.

James V of Scotland
1512–1542

By marrying Mary of Guise, James strengthened Scotland's alliance with the Catholic kingdom of France.

House of Stuart

Mary of Guise
1515–1560

Mary, Queen of Scots
1542–1587

Mary became queen of Scotland when she was just six days old! Later, she tried to take the English throne from Elizabeth I.

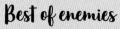

Best of enemies
In this period, the kings and queens of Europe were constantly seeking more power. Alliances and marriages were supposed to keep the peace, but wars often broke out.

Elizabeth of York
1466–1503

Henry's wife was from the House of York. By marrying her, Henry was able to unite the warring country.

The Tudor Rose

Henry VII joined the white rose of York with the red rose of Lancaster to make the Tudor Rose. This marked the union between the two rival houses that, before 1485, had been fighting the Wars of the Roses for more than 30 years.

Traditionally, the throne passed from father to son. A woman could only become queen if there was no male heir.

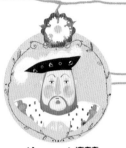

Henry VIII
1491–1547

King Henry had a fiery temper and was good at getting his own way. He replaced Catholicism as England's main religion with his new Church of England.

Henry's wives

Henry VIII married six times, due to various quarrels and his desire to have a male heir. He divorced two of his wives, he had two executed, and one died. His last wife, Katherine Parr, was the only one to survive him.

Katherine of Aragon c.1485–1536	Anne Boleyn c.1507–1536	Jane Seymour c.1509–1537	Anne of Cleves c.1515–1557	Catherine Howard c.1524–1542	Katherine Parr c.1512–1548

Mary Tudor
1496–1533

Mary married the king of France and then, when he died, an English nobleman. She was the grandmother of Lady Jane Grey, who in 1553 became queen of England for nine days.

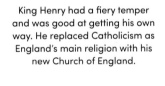

Philip II of Spain
1527–1598

Mary I
1516–1558

Like her Spanish mother, Mary was raised Catholic. When she became queen, she married the king of Spain, and restored Catholicism in England.

Elizabeth I
1533–1603

Elizabeth had a long and exciting life, marked by feuding siblings, legendary battles, and great discoveries.

Edward VI
1537–1553

Edward was a boy king, who came to the throne aged nine. Six years later, he died.

Princess Elizabeth

Elizabeth's childhood was anything but normal. She was the daughter of King Henry VIII, but that didn't mean that things would be easy.

👣 Baby Elizabeth

On September 7, 1533, Queen Anne gave birth to baby Elizabeth in her bedroom at Greenwich Palace. Heralds announced the birth of a new princess, and a grand christening ceremony was held to welcome her into her father's Church of England.

The new baby was mostly cared for by a nurse named Margaret Bryan.

News of Elizabeth's arrival did not excite everyone. Her birth meant that her half-sister Mary was no longer the heir to the throne. Mary refused to curtsey to the new baby or call her "Princess."

King Henry VIII was disappointed to have another daughter. He wanted a son who would one day become king and secure the Tudor dynasty.

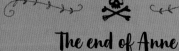

☠ The end of Anne

When Elizabeth was just three years old, Henry ordered her mother Anne to be executed. Thomas Cromwell, one of Henry's advisors, had accused Anne of being unfaithful to Henry.

A new favourite

Just 11 days after Anne's death, Henry VIII married Jane Seymour, and later had the son he always wanted, named Edward. Elizabeth was no longer the heir to the throne, or as important to the king. In fact, she wasn't even called "Princess" anymore, much to Mary's delight.

Edward

At this time, Elizabeth was practically forgotten by Henry. He even had to be reminded to send her new clothes.

A household of servants took care of Elizabeth and Edward.

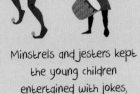

Minstrels and jesters kept the young children entertained with jokes, music, singing, and juggling.

Royal siblings

Elizabeth spent most of her childhood at a large country manor called Hatfield House. Later, Edward came to live with her, and they explored and played in the grounds together.

It wasn't all fun and games. Elizabeth studied hard. She had a personal tutor to teach her how to read and write, and she also learned several languages including Latin, Greek, and French.

By the age of 10, Elizabeth was back in favor with the king. She was added back into the succession, which meant she could one day be queen. But for this to happen, both Edward and Mary would have to die childless.

Journey to the throne

Elizabeth would become one of the greatest rulers in English history, but she was England's most unlikely monarch. Her route to becoming queen had many ups and downs.

3

Troublesome Thomas

When Katherine Parr died in 1548, her husband Thomas Seymour planned to marry Elizabeth as a way to seize the throne. He was eventually executed for plotting against the king, and suspicion fell on Elizabeth, too. She escaped punishment, but her reputation was damaged.

1

Inspiring stepmother

Henry VIII's sixth and final wife, Katherine Parr, was a role model for Elizabeth. Whenever the king was away, Katherine ruled over the royal court, and Elizabeth learned how a strong-minded woman could make powerful men listen.

2

A heavy blow

When Henry VIII died, Elizabeth went to live with Katherine Parr. Her nine-year-old brother Edward became king, but because of his age, the country was run by a squabbling council.

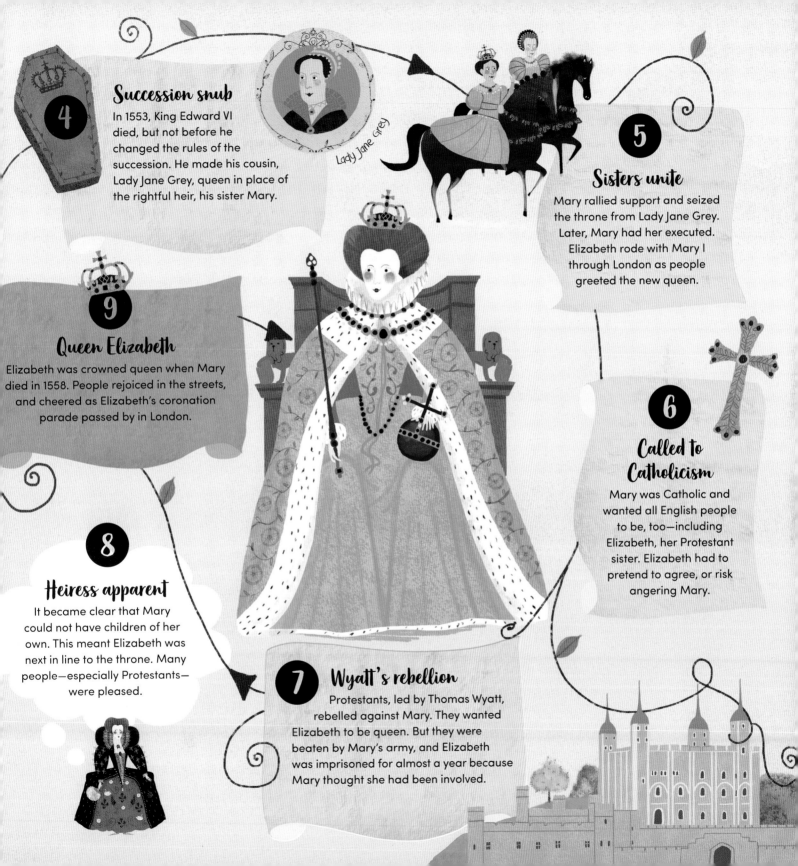

4 Succession snub

In 1553, King Edward VI died, but not before he changed the rules of the succession. He made his cousin, Lady Jane Grey, queen in place of the rightful heir, his sister Mary.

Lady Jane Grey

5 Sisters unite

Mary rallied support and seized the throne from Lady Jane Grey. Later, Mary had her executed. Elizabeth rode with Mary I through London as people greeted the new queen.

9 Queen Elizabeth

Elizabeth was crowned queen when Mary died in 1558. People rejoiced in the streets, and cheered as Elizabeth's coronation parade passed by in London.

6 Called to Catholicism

Mary was Catholic and wanted all English people to be, too—including Elizabeth, her Protestant sister. Elizabeth had to pretend to agree, or risk angering Mary.

8 Heiress apparent

It became clear that Mary could not have children of her own. This meant Elizabeth was next in line to the throne. Many people—especially Protestants—were pleased.

7 Wyatt's rebellion

Protestants, led by Thomas Wyatt, rebelled against Mary. They wanted Elizabeth to be queen. But they were beaten by Mary's army, and Elizabeth was imprisoned for almost a year because Mary thought she had been involved.

A kingdom in crisis

When Elizabeth came to the throne in 1558, England was not doing well. The new queen also had problems of her own to deal with. She knew that her main job was to bring back peace and stability, and to help England become strong once again.

We're poor!

Expensive wars and fancy monarchs had left England £250,000 in debt. (This would be around $87 million in today's money). Elizabeth had to raise money quickly. To make matters worse, bad weather had led to poor harvests, which meant food was more expensive.

We're weak!

England had just lost a war against France and had been forced to give up the only city it controlled in Europe—Calais. Elizabeth knew she needed to strengthen her army and navy.

Anne Boleyn

Should you even be queen?

Some people believed that the marriage between Elizabeth's parents had never been legitimate. To many, Henry's previous marriage to Katherine of Aragon was still valid. This meant that Elizabeth could not be the rightful queen.

Lady Jane Grey

Mary I

You're a woman!

The only queens of England before Elizabeth were Mary I, who was disliked, and Lady Jane Grey, who ruled for nine days. People worried that women couldn't be good leaders. Elizabeth needed to prove them wrong.

You're a Protestant!

Mary had made England Catholic once again. But Catholics did not know what to expect now that Elizabeth, a Protestant, was queen. Elizabeth had the task of settling the religious dispute.

Who will you marry?

Mary's marriage to Philip II of Spain was very unpopular. People were concerned that Elizabeth would also marry a foreigner, and that would allow him to control England.

Catholic allies!

France and Spain were Catholic allies. Together, they could invade England and make Elizabeth's Catholic cousin, Mary, Queen of Scots their chosen queen of England. Elizabeth had to protect herself and her country.

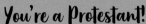

A queen in control

As queen, Elizabeth ruled firmly, and just like her father, she usually got her own way. She was wise and witty, but she could also be short-tempered and ruthless.

Elizabeth's team

To help her rule, Elizabeth chose a group of trusted advisors called the Privy Council. Mary's council had been large and disorderly, but Elizabeth carefully selected 19 people. They met every day and helped Elizabeth make decisions on lots of matters, such as when to go to war or how to raise more money.

Mean queen

Elizabeth had a nasty temper. She was known to punch, kick, spit, or even throw shoes at people who made her angry. She could also write horrible letters to people she didn't like, and give out terrible punishments.

Robert Dudley was Elizabeth's childhood friend and a close advisor.

William Cecil was the Queen's loyal chief advisor. He served her for nearly 50 years.

Francis Walsingham was Elizabeth's spymaster. He used a network of spies to find out about plots against the Queen.

Pesky Parliament

Members of Parliament (MPs) asked the Queen to sort things out in their local areas. But they had very little power. Elizabeth only allowed Parliament to meet 13 times in her entire reign, and she sent one MP to the dungeons just for complaining.

Get rich quick

Elizabeth sold "monopolies," which meant she allowed certain merchants to be the only ones selling particular things. This helped her raise money quickly. But, it meant that merchants could make poor products and still sell them at high prices.

Wrap up, I insist

The wool trade was England's biggest and most important business, and Elizabeth was eager to support it. She even passed a law that required people to wear woolly hats on Sundays.

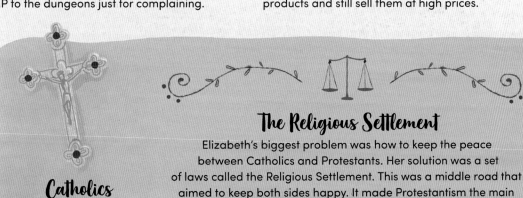

Catholics

The Religious Settlement

Elizabeth's biggest problem was how to keep the peace between Catholics and Protestants. Her solution was a set of laws called the Religious Settlement. This was a middle road that aimed to keep both sides happy. It made Protestantism the main religion in England, but it allowed people to worship in their own way.

Protestants

The Queen on tour

Elizabeth didn't spend all her time in London. She liked to visit her favorite nobles in different parts of the country, on tours called "progresses." When the Queen came to stay, the nobles were very eager to impress her.

Marvelous manors

To show off their wealth, nobles built grand houses, such as Hardwick Hall in Derbyshire, England. There were often separate wings for residents and their servants.

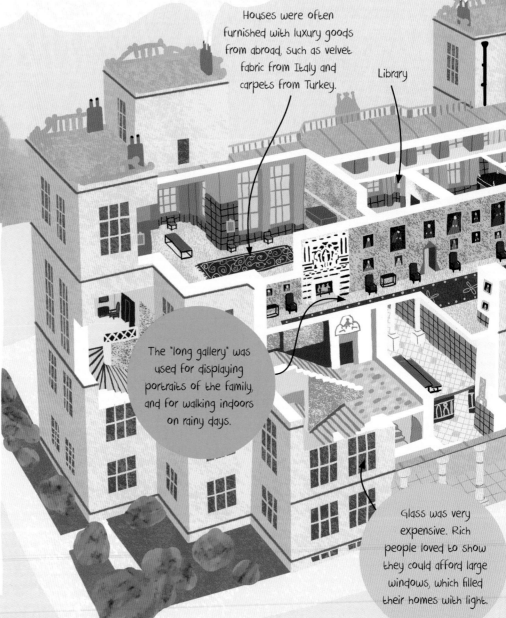

Having several chimneys meant there could be fireplaces throughout the manor.

Houses were often furnished with luxury goods from abroad, such as velvet fabric from Italy and carpets from Turkey.

Library

The "long gallery" was used for displaying portraits of the family, and for walking indoors on rainy days.

Glass was very expensive. Rich people loved to show they could afford large windows, which filled their homes with light.

Top of the tree

Elizabethan society was divided into groups based on wealth. Under the monarch, there were noble families who owned most of the land, and below them were knights.

Fabulous feasts

Lavish banquets were held in Elizabeth's honor, featuring platters of meat, grand pastry creations, and jugs of wine. Elizabeth loved eating sweets, and had rotting, black teeth to show for it.

The Tudors didn't use forks; they ate with knives, spoons, and their fingers.

Mmm, marzipan, my favorite!

Chapel

Kitchen

Come again soon... ish!

Gong farmer

Cleaning up

After the Queen left, a great clean up began. The worst job belonged to the "gong farmer," who had to empty out the toilets.

Showtime

Musicians and jesters performed for the Queen, and shows were held that told stories of great heroes.

Presents

Nobles presented Elizabeth with gifts, such as ornaments, jewelry, or fine clothes to thank her for her stay.

No expense spared

A visit from royalty was an honor, but it could also be very expensive for the host. Elizabeth traveled with her court of around 300 people and 1,000 horses, and they all needed to be taken care of.

Hunting

Elizabeth loved to ride horses and to hunt, too. She often joined the men when they went hunting.

Ordinary life

The rich may have owned all the land, but they were only a tiny part of the population. In the country and in the cities, almost everyone was poor. Elizabeth knew that she needed their support, if her reign was to be long and successful.

In the country

Although the cities were growing quickly, most people were peasants living on farms or in villages. They worked hard from dawn until dusk, growing crops or taking care of animals.

Stinking city

While nobles enjoyed large houses and luxurious lifestyles, the poor lived in terrible conditions. Life in the city was noisy, dirty, and dangerous.

Scavenging birds, such as ravens and red kites, were the only street cleaners in town.

Some families lived together in small apartments. They survived on simple foods such as bread and cheese. Because the water was so dirty, they drank beer.

Crime was common, especially theft. And if criminals got caught, the punishments were severe. They could be put in the stocks, chained to the river bank, or even jailed in the Tower of London's dungeon.

Pigeon pie! Rabbit stew!

Stop, thief!

Click-clack
Click-clack

Entertainment

To pass the time, ordinary people went to the theater, and they played ball games, cards, and dice. They also enjoyed rougher sports such as wrestling, and even watching animals fight.

There were no toilets or sewers, so waste was thrown straight onto the street.

Wooden houses were crammed together on narrow, crooked streets.

Rats were rampant on the dirty streets, and they carried nasty diseases. There were terrible outbreaks of the plague in 1563 and 1589.

Even the Queen wasn't protected from disease. She caught smallpox in 1562, and was left with bad scars and little hair. Because of this, she always wore lots of makeup and a wig.

Common jobs

Elizabeth and her government issued a series of "Poor Laws," which helped poor people who could not work. As for poor people who *could* work, they were forced to do jobs, or else they were sent to prison. Most poor people were unskilled laborers, but others had skilled jobs such as:

Blacksmith

These important workers made weapons and armor out of iron. First, the metal was heated, then hammered into shape on a block called an anvil.

Candlemaker

With no electricity, the only way to light a room after dark was with a candle. Candlemakers were skilled at making candles using an animal fat called tallow, and they could make torches and lanterns, too.

Barber

Just like today, Elizabethan barbers cut hair. But without many doctors or dentists around, they could also be asked to perform surgery or pull out sore teeth!

Finest fashion

Wealthy Elizabethans loved to dress up, and none more so than Elizabeth. Servants helped the Queen into fabulous clothes and made sure she looked the part. From start to finish, it could take four hours to get ready!

Face makeup

Elizabeth wore lots of makeup to cover up the scars on her face. But the white powder she used was made with toxic lead, which made her skin worse. Her red lipstick contained another poisonous metal called mercury.

Elizabeth wore a red wig made from human hair.

Each sleeve had to be attached separately.

A stiff frame called a farthingale held the skirt out wide.

A gown made from soft sable fur kept Elizabeth warm.

Fine fabrics were colored using exotic dyes and embroidered with silver or gold thread.

A silk or velvet corset was fitted tight to the upper body.

A pomander was filled with cinnamon, cloves, and other scents to keep away bad smells. The pomander was also believed to ward off nasty diseases.

Elizabeth forbade anyone except royalty from wearing the color purple.

Dashing dudes

Looking good was important to rich men, too. They wore extravagant outfits that showed off their status, and made them look confident and impressive.

This pleated collar, called a ruff, was stiffened with a substance called starch.

The doublet was a tight jacket made from wool or leather. Underneath, men wore silk shirts with frilly cuffs.

Some men wore an accessory called a codpiece.

Foreign treasures

Items from far away places were in high demand. Gold, silver, and precious gems were made into glittering jewelry. To make clothes in exciting new colors, dyes such as cochineal and indigo were needed.

Ordinary people

Most people in Elizabethan England weren't wealthy. They couldn't afford fancy clothes, and in any case, they weren't allowed to wear them. The law said that only nobles could wear bright colors and fine fabrics, so peasants wore dull clothes.

Layers were important to stay warm in chilly England.

Felt hat

Long socks or woollen hose

The hose was tight around the lower legs, but puffed out with horsehair higher up.

Velvet slipper-like shoes were popular.

Royal rivals

Elizabeth was a popular queen, but she had enemies, too. Her main rival was her own cousin, Mary, Queen of Scots, who believed she was the rightful queen of England.

Tudor blood

Mary was the great-granddaughter of Henry VII. Many people thought Mary had a stronger claim to the throne, because they believed Elizabeth's father and mother should never have been allowed to marry or have children.

Catholic support

Mary was a Catholic, and the Catholics in England supported her because they disliked Elizabeth's Protestant ways.

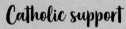

Foreign friends

Spain and France were both very powerful Catholic countries that wanted to replace Elizabeth with Mary. They encouraged secret plots to overthrow the Queen, and promised to support revolts.

Four and out

Elizabeth knew that executing Mary would anger France and Spain, so in 1568, Elizabeth imprisoned her instead. From 1569–1586, Mary and her supporters tried to overthrow Elizabeth four times.

The Northern Rising
1569

Powerful Catholic earls managed to take over parts of northern England, but Elizabeth's army fought back.

The Ridolfi Plot
1571

A spy named Roberto Ridolfi plotted to kill Elizabeth and have Spanish troops invade England, but his plan was unsuccessful.

The Babington Plot
1586

Letters between Anthony Babington and Mary, Queen of Scots discussing a plan to overthrow Elizabeth were found. Elizabeth had had enough. After 19 years in prison, Mary, Queen of Scots was put on trial and executed in 1587.

The Throckmorton Plot
1583

A French duke, the king of Spain, and the Pope joined forces with a man named Francis Throckmorton and plotted to invade England and replace Elizabeth with Mary. Luckily, Francis Walsingham and his network of spies uncovered the plan before it was carried out.

Catholic crackdown

With every plot against her, Elizabeth became less trusting of Catholics. As time went on, she began punishing and even executing Catholic priests. Some used secret hiding places called priest holes to try to avoid Elizabeth's soldiers.

Priest holes were built in fireplaces, staircases, and attics.

The next generation

Before she died, Mary had a child named James. He became king of Scotland, and eventually king of England after Elizabeth died. His mother would have been proud.

Birth of an empire

Throughout the 1500s, Spain and Portugal had been traveling the world, invading foreign countries, and bringing great riches back home. When Elizabeth came to the throne, England was weak and poor in comparison. That, she decided, had to change.

The Queen's pirates

Privateers were fierce sailors who raided foreign ports and captured enemy ships carrying huge amounts of treasure. They were a lot like pirates, but unlike them, privateers had support from the crown—Elizabeth even called them her "sea dogs." With their help, Elizabeth was able to seize treasures from Spanish ships.

Heading westward

One of Elizabeth's sea dogs, Walter Raleigh, sailed to North America and established an English community on Roanoke Island. Although it was short-lived, this was England's first settlement abroad. In future years, Britain would become wealthy through ruling parts of America and other lands around the world.

Francis Drake's historic voyage took place aboard the Golden Hind.

Around the world

Elizabeth paid one of her favorite sea dogs, Francis Drake, to lead the first English voyage around the world. Drake found new lands and raided ships as he went. When he returned three years later, he had enough treasure to give Elizabeth 47 times the amount she had paid him.

Hit and miss

Expeditions didn't always work out. The sailor Martin Frobisher tried (and failed) three times to find the Northwest Passage—a route to Asia over the top of North America. He brought back a huge amount of rock that he thought contained gold, but was actually worthless.

A divider was used to mark a ship's position at sea.

Sailors used a compass to find their way at sea.

Mapping the world

As well as improving English ships, Elizabeth recognized the need for accurate maps. She chose the mathematician John Dee as the court astronomer, and he developed the fields of mapmaking and navigation. This helped English sailors explore the world more easily.

A fine fleet

During Elizabeth's reign, the English navy grew stronger. A new type of galleon ship (warship) that was faster, niftier, and could carry more guns was built. Soon England had a fleet of 23 ships that could rival the Spanish at sea.

The Spanish Armada

In 1588, Elizabeth faced a terrible threat. King Philip II of Spain was fed up with English raids on his treasure-filled ships. Also, he had long wanted to restore Catholicism in England. He launched the Spanish Armada—the largest fleet of ships in the world—to conquer England.

Plan of attack

The Spanish fleet was made up of around 150 ships and 19,000 soldiers. The plan was to collect 30,000 more men from the Spanish Netherlands, and together they would defeat the English navy and invade England.

English navy

Spanish Armada

Legend has it that Francis Drake was playing a game of bowls when he heard that the Armada had reached England.

Spain

Ireland

Scotland

England

At this time, Wales was part of the kingdom of England.

Plymouth

4 Many ships were caught in storms around the north and west coasts of the British Isles.

1

Sea change

The defeat of the Armada was a turning point in world history. Mighty Spain was weakened, and the English navy ruled the seas. Soon, England would have an empire of its own.

The English had better ships, with bigger cannons.

3

2

Calais

Spanish Netherlands

France

How the Armada was defeated

Crescent shape

1 Early battles

The Spanish fleet sailed in a strong crescent shape, which made it difficult to attack. The English followed the Armada up the English Channel, firing long-range guns to try to inflict damage.

2 Waiting for support

The Armada anchored near the port of Calais in France. There, they waited for the army from the Spanish Netherlands to join them. But while they stayed still they were vulnerable to attack.

3 Fireship ambush

That night, the English set fire to their old ships and sent them drifting toward the Armada. Some Spanish ships collided as they fled, and the Armada's formation was broken. In the morning, the English gunboats fired at the Spanish fleet.

4 Fleeing in fear

The Spanish commander ordered his ships to retreat, but there was nowhere to go except north. On the long route back to Spain, many ships were wrecked in storms. Only 65 made it home.

William Shakespeare

One of the world's most famous writers, William Shakespeare was born in 1564 in Stratford-upon-Avon, England. He was a brilliant storyteller, and wrote nearly 40 plays as well as hundreds of poems. He also acted, and was a part-owner of the Globe Theatre.

Shakespeare's theater

Welcome, welcome! This is the Globe Theatre in London, where locals crammed in to see plays by their favorite Elizabethan writer, William Shakespeare. It was cheap, it was fun, and it could get quite rowdy!

Opened in 1599, the original Globe burned down in 1613. A replica was later built on the same site.

Costumes gave the audience a clue to the characters' social status.

The rich sat in the galleries, while poorer people stood in an area around the stage called "the pit." Here, tickets cost a penny.

At this time, all actors were male. Boys even played the female roles.

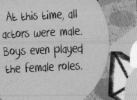

Royal approval

Elizabeth loved the theater and helped it grow. She asked drama companies to perform for her at court, and encouraged other people to attend plays.

There were no lights, so performances always took place during the day.

There was no roof. If it rained, you got wet!

It could be noisy, as people talked, ate, and moved around. They cheered, booed, and sometimes threw things at the performers.

There was little background scenery. The focus was on the actors.

Types of play

To be, or not to be...

Tragedy

These sad and powerful plays involve struggles, destruction, and death. The main character has a flaw, such as Hamlet's inability to make important decisions in the play of the same name.

The course of true love never did run smooth...

Comedy

Shakespeare wrote comic plays to make people laugh. They tell of love, mishaps, and magic, such as *A Midsummer Night's Dream*, in which a character named Puck plays magical tricks on people.

My kingdom for a horse!

History

Shakespeare's histories tell the tales of English kings, but he often twisted the facts to make a good story. In *Richard III*, the main character schemes and tells lies to gain the throne.

Pros

Elizabeth felt that marriage might cause as many problems as it would solve. By staying single she could:

 Keep complete control of decisions

 Make sure that England stayed free from foreign influence

 Remain free to influence the leaders of other countries

Single and strong

Most people expected Elizabeth to get married and have children, but the Queen had other ideas. She saw the strength in staying single and independent, particularly for her country's sake.

X Robert Dudley

Robert was Elizabeth's childhood friend, but he was already married. When his wife died suddenly, some people thought he was involved in her death. This damaged his reputation and Elizabeth had to distance herself from him.

Dudley built a garden to impress Elizabeth. When she complained she couldn't see it from her room, he made his gardeners move it!

X Philip II, King of Spain

Shortly after Mary I died, her husband, Philip II, proposed to Mary's sister, Elizabeth. The new queen knew he was unpopular in England, so she rejected the offer.

Charles II, Archduke of Austria

Charles was a member of the powerful Habsburg family of Austria, who ruled an empire in central Europe. But he was a Catholic, and Elizabeth didn't want to risk dividing England by religion again.

Francis the French Duke

Elizabeth suggested that she might marry Francis, so that she could influence what happened in France. But she was growing old. Elizabeth knew if she married Francis and then died, the Frenchman could seize control of England.

Cons

Elizabeth was aware that there was a downside to staying single. She knew it would mean:

 There would be no Tudor heir to the throne

 England would miss out on gaining a strong ally

 Rivals might think she was weak and could be overthrown

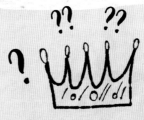

No husband, no heir

Elizabeth never did marry or have a child. Still, she was determined to ensure a smooth succession. She decided the throne would pass to her cousin and the son of Mary, Queen of Scots—King James VI of Scotland.

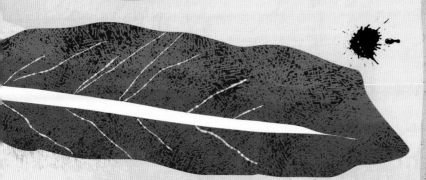

Elizabeth's lifetime

Elizabeth I was queen for 45 years, leading England through troubled times into an exciting new period. Throughout her life, she had to overcome countless challenges, fight off enemies, and prove her doubters wrong.

1533
Elizabeth is born in London, England. Her father is King Henry VIII, her mother is Anne Boleyn, and her half-sister is Mary.

1553
Edward dies. After a brief power struggle, Mary becomes the new queen.

1558
Mary I dies, and Elizabeth becomes queen of England. She is 25 years old.

How can we overthrow her?

1568
Elizabeth's cousin and main rival, Mary, Queen of Scots, comes to England. Elizabeth keeps a close eye on her and her supporters, who are plotting rebellions.

1580
With Elizabeth's support, the explorer Francis Drake completes an incredible round-the-world trip. He returns with lots of treasure.

1588
The king of Spain sends a huge fleet called the Spanish Armada to conquer England. Elizabeth's navy defeats it and saves the country from invasion.

1598
Elizabeth's closest advisor, William Cecil, dies after serving the Queen for 40 years. His son, Robert, takes over as Elizabeth's chief minister.

1599
The Globe Theatre opens in London. Many of William Shakespeare's plays are first performed at the Globe.

1603
Elizabeth dies after a short illness. She is buried in Westminster Abbey in London, next to her half-sister Mary.

1536

Henry VIII has Anne Boleyn put to death, and marries another woman named Jane Seymour.

1537

Elizabeth's half-brother Edward is born, and his mother Jane Seymour dies shortly after giving birth.

1547

Elizabeth's father, Henry VIII, dies. Edward becomes the new king, aged nine.

1584

Another explorer, Walter Raleigh, goes on an expedition to North America to set up England's first settlement abroad.

1587

Elizabeth orders the execution of Mary, Queen of Scots, who had been a constant threat.

Good Queen Bess

Elizabeth is fondly remembered by many as "Good Queen Bess"—a wise and determined woman who stood up for herself and her country.

A golden age?

Many people think Elizabeth's reign was one of England's most successful periods, and Elizabeth was even nicknamed "Gloriana" meaning "glorious one." But in truth there were still many problems, such as poverty and war.

After Elizabeth

Elizabeth never had children, so the Tudor dynasty came to an end and a new era began. Her achievements laid the foundations for England to grow and prosper, and her reign would be remembered forever.

English Civil War
1642–1651

This was one of England's most difficult periods. King Charles I was defeated by Oliver Cromwell in 1651, and after this there were no kings or queens of England until 1660.

House of Hanover
1714–1901

Queen Anne had no children, so the throne passed to her relatives in the Hanover family from Germany. More than 300 years later, the British royal family is still going strong.

House of Stuart
1371–1714

Following Elizabeth's wishes, the crown passed to James VI of Scotland, who then became James I of England. The new ruling family were named the Stuarts.

Charles II
1660–1685

James II
1685–1688

A united kingdom

James was the first king of both England and Scotland. This began a union that eventually developed into the United Kingdom of Great Britain and Northern Ireland, or the UK.

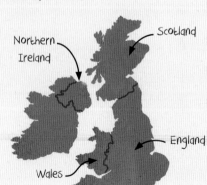

Northern Ireland
Scotland
England
Wales

Charles I
1625–1649

James (VI and I)
1567–1625

Anne
1702–1714

William III and Mary II
1689–1702

After James II fled England, the throne was passed to his daughter Mary, who ruled with her Dutch husband, William. They gave more power to Parliament, and passed a law saying that all future monarchs should be Protestant.